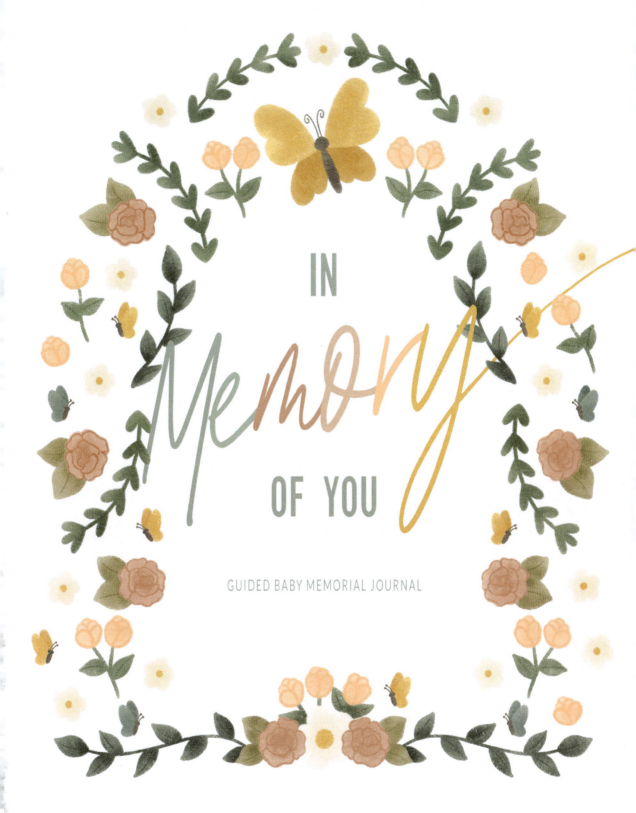

Copyright © 2022 Autumn Cohen All rights reserved.

This book is protected by the copyright laws of the United States of America. This book may not be copied or reprinted for commercial gain or profit. The use of short quotations or occasional page copying for personal or group study is encouraged. Permission will be granted upon request from Autumn Cohen.

Library of Congress Control Number: 2022921157

ISBN: 979-8-9872987-0-1 Hardcover
       979-8-9872987-1-8 Paperback

Published by Rebel Queen

In loving memory of you,

_____

Born on

_____

Due on

_____

This book is dedicated to my little guy in the sky,
Bastion Porter Cohen

And his heavenly best friends-
Baby Garaffa, Carson Cloutier,
Edith Barry, Harvey de Witte,
Henry Fitzpatrick, Joseph Grant,
& Robert John Bruns

To my husband, Brandon, and my daughters, Adeline & Colbie

Hello fellow grievers.

I am truly sorry for your loss.

This journal is designed for you as you embark on this grief journey and process the loss of your precious baby. Use this tool in any order as you see fit. Grief is not linear.

Throughout this experience, you may smile, find contentment, and will surely shed tears. I hope journaling helps you find a connection with your baby during this process. Years from now, I hope you look back on your entries and feel a closeness with your beautiful child. Your thoughts and feelings in the present may not be what you think and feel in the future. When you revisit this journal, your raw and unfiltered pain will be a marker to illustrate how far you have come. Still missing your child, but oh so strong and courageous.

These feelings and memories are immeasurable. When we lose our future with our children, our past becomes integral to keeping their memory and love alive.

With love,
Autumn, Bash's mama

Suggestions From A Licensed Therapist

You've experienced a grief that not everyone can understand. Autumn is someone who does and created this book to help you process what you've been through. She holds your hand as you reflect on the moments you had and didn't get to have. She knows what it's like. I hope this brings you comfort and helps you feel less alone in your pain.

However, I want to remind you to pace yourself, to know when to open the book and when to put it down. Consider what might help you as you write down your thoughts. Do you need a hand to hold? Someone to sit by you? A timer to go off every 10 minutes to remind you to take a breath?

Many of us were not taught how to process grief, even though it is an experience we will all have at some point, though our grief is not all the same. Your grief may look like sadness, feel like an aching in the chest, or make you feel like you can't breathe. It may be heavy like a weight or perhaps you're completely numb.

When you've lost someone you love, especially a child, it is common to yearn to be with them, to maybe wish you could be where they are, to switch places. It can feel unbearable at times to go on living when you can't be with your baby in the way you want to be. Those thoughts and feelings are understandable and are often more intense shortly after the loss. They may come and go over time and they may get quieter or less intense. However, if you are considering acting on those thoughts please immediately reach out to a therapist who specializes in infant loss. In fact, even if you're not having those thoughts it typically can't hurt to talk to a therapist about your experience. You deserve that kind of support.

It is said that grief is love with nowhere to go. This book will hopefully provide you a place to express the love you have for your baby. Let this process also be about providing love to yourself. You deserve to be held while you hold the memory of your baby in the sky.

Erin Spahr, LCPC, LCMHC, PMH-C
Certified Perinatal Mental Health Therapist
www.erinspahrtherapy.com
Instagram @feminist.mom.therapist
erin@erinspahrtherapy.com

Find a Therapist:
https://psidirectory.com/listing/perinatal-loss
https://rtzhope.org/counseling-us

"IF I HAD A FLOWER FOR EVERY TIME I THOUGHT OF YOU...
I COULD WALK THROUGH MY GARDEN FOREVER."

Alfred Tennyson

Table Of Contents

PREGNANCY WITH YOU	01
YOUR ARRIVAL	21
FAMILY & FRIENDS JOURNALING	28
YOUR GOODBYE STORY	41
WHAT COULD HAVE BEEN	51
LIFE AFTER LOSING YOU	59
BIG MOMENTS WITHOUT YOU	72
HONORING YOU	83
CELEBRATING YOU	93
VALIDATING MY GRIEF	107
OPEN JOURNALING	116
DEAR FUTURE ME	126
DEAR PAST ME	129

Forever My Baby You'll Be Picture Page

The Littlest Feet Leave The Biggest Imprint

Sending My Love

No rules, just write what comes to mind.

Dear

CHAPTER ONE
PREGNANCY WITH YOU

Congrats To Us!

Place an ultrasound photo here

YOU WERE

☐ PLANNED

☐ A SURPRISE

WE THOUGHT YOU'D BE

☐ A GIRL

☐ A BOY

☐ UNSURE

NAMES WE LIKED, BUT DIDN'T USE

Describe the journey of becoming pregnant.

First Trimester
Picture Page

IST TRIMESTER
0–12 WEEKS

We found out we were pregnant on

What memories stand out from this time?

Second Trimester
Picture Page

2ND TRIMESTER
12-24 WEEKS

We entered the 2nd trimester on

What memories stand out from this time?

Third Trimester
Picture Page

3RD TRIMESTER
24 – 40+ WEEKS

We entered the 3rd trimester on

(or would have entered on)

What memories stand out from this time?

First photo from pregnancy

(Or first photo of baby)

4x4 inches

Last photo from pregnancy

(Or last photo of baby)

4x4 inches

A Glimpse Into Pregnancy

Was pregnancy textbook standard or anything but?

Any wild dreams?

Unique cravings or food aversions?

Classes, books, or other things we did to prepare...

The Big Reveal

Gender Reveal · Baby Announcement

How we announced our pregnancy and/or revealed your gender...

Showered With Love

Baby Shower Picture Page

Details of your baby shower or what it could have looked like...

Hush Little Baby

Baby or Nursery Picture Page

Your nursery theme...

The process of putting away, donating, and displaying your clothes and other belongings...

You Are My Sunshine

A reason I have smiled because of you...

You got this big!
Circle the gestational week delivered.

apple seed
5 weeks

sweet pea
6 weeks

blueberry
7 weeks

raspberry
8 weeks

grape
9 weeks

prune
10 weeks

lime
11 weeks

plum
12 weeks

peach
13 weeks

lemon
14 weeks

apple
15 weeks

avacado
16 weeks

pear
17 weeks

sweet potato
18 weeks

mango
19 weeks

banana
20 weeks

pomegrantate
21 weeks

papaya
22 weeks

grapefruit
23 weeks

cantaloupe
24 weeks

cauliflower
25 weeks

lettuce
26 weeks

rutabaga
27 weeks

eggplant
28 weeks

acorn squash
29 weeks

cabbage
30 weeks

pineapple
31 weeks

jicama
32 weeks

durian
33 weeks

butternut squash
34 weeks

coconut
35 weeks

honeydew
36 weeks

winter melon
37 weeks

pumpkin
38 weeks

watermelon
39 weeks

jackfruit
40+ weeks

CHAPTER TWO
YOUR ARRIVAL

Due With You

WE HAD YOU

○ before our due date.
○ after our due date.
○ on our due date.

Our due date was on

How was this day?

Grown In Loving Memory

This is your special month, my baby.

Circle the birth month flower...

THE STORY OF YOUR NAME

Every Baby Deserves A Birth Certificate

CERTIFICATE OF RECOGNITION

First Name of Child

Middle & Last Name

Date of Birth

Name of Hospital

Address of Hospital

Name of Parent: First & Last, Relation to Child

Name of Parent: First & Last, Relation to Child

Your Mailing Address

Signature

Your Birth Story

AS TOLD BY:

Photo of you & me

4x6 inches

Your Birth Story AS TOLD BY:

The two of us
4x6 inches

Your Birth Story   AS TOLD BY:

Use this page to write a comforting note in honor of the baby.

Your Birth Story AS TOLD BY:

Use this page to write a comforting note in honor of the baby.

Your Birth Story   AS TOLD BY:

Use this page to write a comforting note in honor of the baby.

Your Birth Story

AS TOLD BY:

Use this page to write a comforting note in honor of the baby.

Baby Stats

DATE

TIME

WEIGHT

HEIGHT

What makes you beautiful...

What I didn't expect when I first saw you...

Who you look like...

My favorite part about you...

Were there any regrets from the time spent in the hospital?

Describe the first day home from the hospital...

Here For A Moment

What was the reason for the hospital visit?

What is a random memory from that day?

Describe the laboring experience.

Loved For A Lifetime

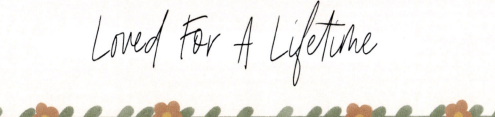

What it felt like holding you for the first time...

A memory that stands out from those first moments...

The room looked and felt like...

My connection with you...

Who came to meet you...

Gone, But Not Forgotten

Urn or Gravesite Photo Page

☐ Cremation
☐ Burial

Dates to remember (examples: your service, coming home, final resting place):
_____
_____

Moments to never forget:
_____
_____

A song to remember you by:
_____
_____

Your most cherished items:
_____
_____

Special gifts, flowers, donations:
_____
_____

i miss you   i miss yo

forever my baby   forever my baby

CHAPTER THREE
YOUR GOODBYE STORY

How I Grieve You

- ☐ Cried in bed
- ☐ Ate comfort food
- ☐ Didn't eat enough
- ☐ Talked to a therapist
- ☐ Joined online support groups
- ☐ Joined a support group in person
- ☐ Visited your grave
- ☐ Got you a special urn
- ☐ Read a book about grieving
- ☐ Bought a weighted teddy bear to hold
- ☐ Bought something to remember you by
- ☐ Listened to a podcast
- ☐ Found others like me
- ☐ Looked through my pregnancy photos
- ☐ Made a playlist
- ☐ Prayed
- ☐ Started a new hobby
- ☐ Supported others like me
- ☐ Cried some more
- ☐ Made a shadow box
- ☐ Looked at photos of you
- ☐ Made a memory box
- ☐ Vented to a friend
- ☐ Bought something for you

Grief Is My Love With No Where To Go

Expanded thoughts from the checklist.

The Story Of Losing You

Yell at this page. Cry over the words written. This is hard— the absolute hardest. Remember that this is your story; if it isn't meant to be written, rip this page out. Sending love and support.

How others are grieving you...

Moments That Last

From the last kicks to the final family moments, describe some memories here.

Not Your Typical "Baby's Firsts"

We experience our own "firsts" after our baby's "lasts."
The first time shopping for groceries, visiting family, or returning to work.
Describe some of those first moments here.

CHAPTER FOUR
WHAT COULD HAVE BEEN

Getting To Know My Grown-Ups

Special things you should know about us...

I am your...

I am your...

A special place for a special photo

4x6in

Dreaming of a life we could have had...

CHAPTER FIVE
LIFE AFTER LOSING YOU

How I Cherish You

cherish /CHeriSH/ verb
Protect and care for (someone) lovingly

Similar: adore, hold dear, love, treasure

Our mama & papa bear instincts have nowhere to go after this loss. We cherish you by holding on a bit longer, protecting your legacy, and loving you deeply.

- ☐ Light a candle
- ☐ Look for rainbows
- ☐ Collect keepsakes
- ☐ Hug our teddy bear
- ☐ Got a tattoo
- ☐ Find pictures in clouds
- ☐ Wear special jewelry
- ☐ Watch for butterflies
- ☐ Grow a garden
- ☐ Look for red cardinals
- ☐ Write letters to you
- ☐ Talk about you

Other ways I cherish you...

_____
_____
_____
_____

I Will Love You Forever

Expanded thoughts from the checklist.

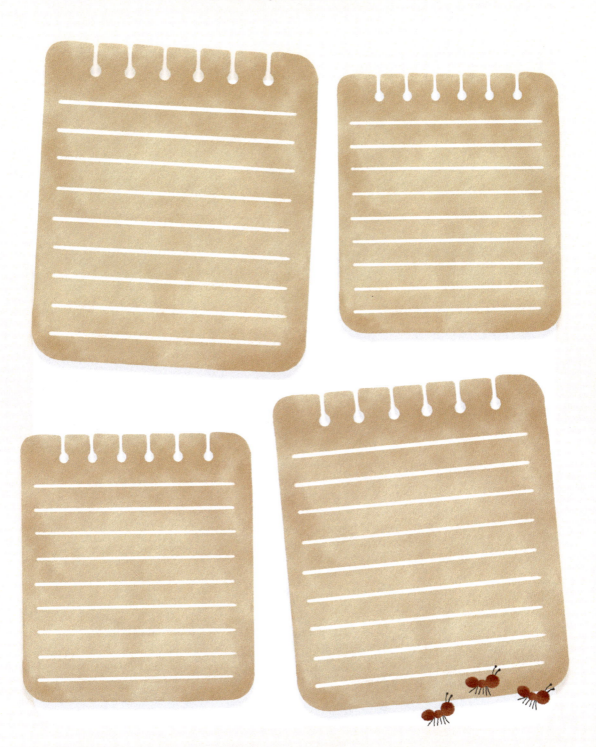

I think of you when...

What comforts me...

What I'll always remember the most about you...

What I wish to tell you...

I saw something & thought you'd like it...

Things around the house that are yours...

If I could hear your voice, the first thing I'd want you to say is...

Some signs you have sent me...

Missing You A Little More Today

A page for when I'm desperately asking, "Why did this happen; why me?"

Words Of Wisdom

Keep inspirational & motivational messages to remember here.

Figuring Out My New "Normal"

A page for when it's time to go back to work or revisit an old routine.

Today Is Just For Me

A page for when getting out of bed is impossible.

A Glimpse Of Happiness

Describe an unexpected bit of happy.

Zzz...

A page for when sleep just isn't going to happen.

Just A Bunch Of Cuties
Family Photos

Siblings That Came Before & After You

Pets make great siblings too! Have each sibling either draw a picture, write a message, or stamp their hand (or paw) & sign. Dedicate these sweet mementos to their forever baby. Remember to add the date!

Big Moments Without You

What are some feelings surrounding these occasions? How are others acting?
Does it feel like a traditional celebration, or does avoiding the festivities feel more natural?

The first birthday without you was

Date:

My first holiday without you was

Date:

My first big trip without you was

Date:

Another holiday without you was

Date:

A celebration without you was

Date:

Another big event without you was

Date:

The first baby born after you was

Date:

Another event without you was

Lyrics, Poems, & Quotes

...that remind me of you.

Playlist

In the spaces below, write comforting songs, podcasts, or audiobooks.

CHAPTER SIX
HONORING YOU

How I Honor You

- ☐ Started something new
- ☐ Created a space for baby
- ☐ Participate in charity events
- ☐ Plant flowers
- ☐ Started a social media account
- ☐ Volunteer
- ☐ Continue to speak your name
- ☐ Fight to make the world a better place
- ☐ Display reminders of you
- ☐ _____
- ☐ Acts of kindness
- ☐ Donate to charity
- ☐ Planted trees
- ☐ Created your legacy
- ☐ Started a blog
- ☐ Celebrated your birthday
- ☐ Strive to be my best self
- ☐ Talk about you
- ☐ Meditate
- ☐ Educate others on preventing loss

Share more about a favorite...

_____
_____
_____
_____

My Heart Is With You

Expanded thoughts from the checklist.

Self-care regimens that help the most...

*Is there anything positive that has come from this journey?
If not, visit page 44 and return to this one later.*

A location that sparks a feeling of connection with you...

How others send comfort when grief feels heavy...

Just Makes Sense

This is how certain senses spark memories of you, whether positive or negative...

SIGHTS & THINGS UNSEEN

_____
_____
_____
_____
_____
_____

SCENTS & SMELLS

_____
_____
_____
_____
_____
_____

SOUNDS & THINGS HEARD

_____
_____
_____
_____
_____
_____

TASTE & FOODS

_____
_____
_____
_____
_____
_____

TOUCH & FEEL

_____
_____
_____
_____

New Things In My Life

...I wish I could share with you.

CHAPTER SEVEN
CELEBRATING YOU

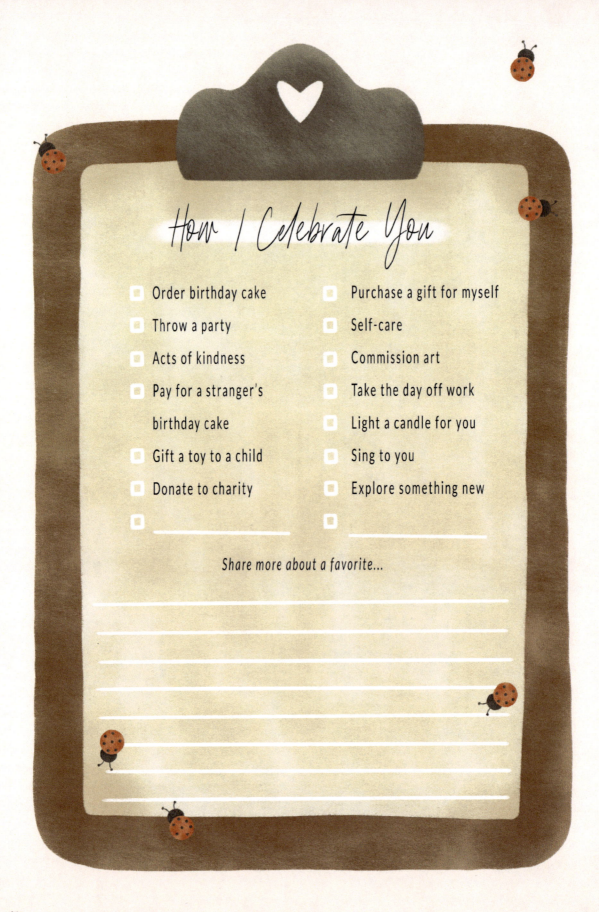

How I Celebrate You

- ☐ Order birthday cake
- ☐ Throw a party
- ☐ Acts of kindness
- ☐ Pay for a stranger's birthday cake
- ☐ Gift a toy to a child
- ☐ Donate to charity
- ☐ _____

- ☐ Purchase a gift for myself
- ☐ Self-care
- ☐ Commission art
- ☐ Take the day off work
- ☐ Light a candle for you
- ☐ Sing to you
- ☐ Explore something new
- ☐ _____

Share more about a favorite...

It's Your Special Day

Expanded thoughts from the checklist.

Monthly (Missed) Milestones

What I did or how I reflected during your first year...

One month

1

Two months

2

Three months

3

Four months

4

Five months

5

Your Half Birthday

What I did or how I reflected...

Seven months

7 _____

_____

_____

_____

_____

_____

Eight months

8 _____

_____

_____

_____

_____

_____

Nine months

9 _____

_____

_____

_____

_____

_____

_____

Ten months

10 _____

_____

_____

_____

_____

_____

_____

Eleven months

11 _____

_____

_____

_____

_____

_____

_____

Happy First Birthday To You

What I did or how I reflected...

Anniversary Reflection

Whether it's been a year after birth, a year after losing you, or an anniversary of any number that needs reflecting, write what has changed. What has felt better? What has been worse?

Birthday traditions just for you...

My biggest wish...

A Gentle Happy Birthday

Write how these birthdays were celebrated or reflected...

2 years old

3 years old

4 years old

5 years old

6 years old

7 years old

8 years old

9 years old

10 years old

11 years old

12 years old

13 years old

14 years old

15 years old

16 years old

17 years old

18 years old

19 years old

20 years old

21 years old

CHAPTER EIGHT
VALIDATING MY GRIEF

Support System Checklist

I have at least one person...
- ☐ I can vent to with no retaliations
- ☐ I trust with all my heart
- ☐ Who lets me grieve my way

If it feels like there is nowhere to go with this tremendous grief, please seek help from a therapist.

Look for green flags from people all around.

I have someone in my life who...
- ☐ Has a calming presence
- ☐ Respects me
- ☐ Listens without judgement
- ☐ Is supportive
- ☐ Makes an effort
- ☐ Makes me feel valued
- ☐ Gives me space when it's needed

It's understandable to avoid these when in a funk...

- Social media
- New movies or shows
- Friends that don't have our best interest in mind
- Baby showers
- Meeting newborns

Disconnecting from the internet can provide a shield from possible unforeseen triggers.

A safe person validates feelings, listens, and provides comfort when talking or texting.

Ideas to help calm myself...

- Take a shower or bath
- Venture outside
- Take a short walk
- Talk to a safe person
- Seek help from a therapist
- Meditate
- Listen to music
- Read a book

Love Notes To You

Sweet messages to you, my baby.

Love Notes To Me

Write words of affirmation.

What is something unexpected from grieving?

Share tips on how to get through the most challenging days...

What are some of the biggest struggles these days?   Date:

What are some things people should stop saying?

Use these following pages as open journaling. Is today a big day or just a day like any other?

Are there any particular frustrations or happy moments?

Today is   *and I am feeling...*

Today is   *and I am feeling...*

Today is   *and I am feeling...*

Today is   and I am feeling...

Today is   and I am feeling...

Today is   and I am feeling...

Today is   and I am feeling...

Today is   and I am feeling...

Today is   and I am feeling...

Today is   and I am feeling...

What have these past few days, weeks, or months looked liked? What is there to look forward to? Use this space to capture current feelings, stresses, and thoughts. These emotions can evolve in surprising ways.

Today's Date:

Dear Future Me,

This is a time to reflect. There has been growth and many changes, maybe some setbacks. What have these past few years looked liked?

Today's Date:

Dear Past Me,

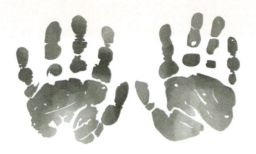

Bastion Porter Cohen

MARCH 25, 2020

Our baby, Bash, was stillborn in Harbor City, California. He died suddenly, days after a normal 37-week appointment. He is our middle child and only son. Bastion was so beautiful, born sleeping peacefully. Our hearts continue to ache for him.

In honor of him, we created Still Loved, a foundation celebrating the birthdays of babies who earned their wings too soon—sending cards to cherish angel babies every year when others seem to forget. Sign up for your card at Still-Loved.org.

You can also find printable resources, like the Certificate of Recognition, to go alongside this journal at BabyLossBook.com.

Sending hugs to you all!

Autumn Cohen
Bash's Mama

Bash's hands & feet are illustrated by Stephanie Grant
LittleTeardropCo.com

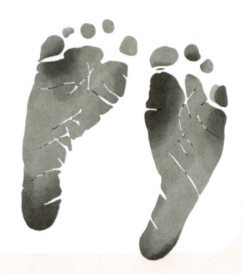

Made in the USA
Monee, IL
16 August 2024

c3ed8a2f-607f-49bf-a879-292a6c8d5ec1R01